# THE STORY OF THE
# Acadians

*by*
*Amy Boudreau*

**PELICAN PUBLISHING COMPANY**
GRETNA 1997

Library of Congress Catalog No. 78-173469
ISBN: 911116-30-3
Manufactured in the United States of America
Published by Pelican Publishing Company, Inc.
1101 Monroe Street, Gretna, Louisiana 70053

# Foreword

Consulat Général de France

La Nouvelle Orléans

1228 WHITNEY BLDG.

TELEPHONE: MAgnolia 6821

The poem written by Miss Amy Boudreau is a timely and appropriate hommage to the French ancestors of the Acadian people of Louisiana.

She has, in poetical terms which at times approach the epic, related the unforgettable and immortal story of the Acadian people, their sufferings, their unfailing courage and their staunch faith in their destiny because of their unshakable belief in God.

I hope that many will read this poem and appreciate the message it contains: a message of affectionate admiration for their French ancestors and one of loving loyalty to the great American nation of which they are now a part.

New Orleans, Louisiana, October 11, 1955.

Guy Quoniam de Schompré,
Consul General of France.

3

Old French map of Nova Scotia
dated 1700

Note original spelling, "Acadie".

4

# CHAPTER ONE

I ponder the question this star-strewn night:
Of what? Of when? Of whom should I write?

I would write of some happening—something fine
That has taken place in this land of mine.

Something outstanding and set apart
That stirs the pulse and touches the heart.

Something that happened once long ago,
but lingers on like an afterglow.

There is much, so much, to write about,
I could write for days and not run out

Of things to say. For, though it is young,
My country's praise is often sung.

Must I tell how we conquered a wilderness?
Of our years of battle, and strife and stress?

How we leveled forests, and built new homes?
And churches with steeples and spires and domes?

How we planted fields and built up flocks?
And sailed our ships to strang, far docks?

We were never aggressive – that I'll say –
But our boundary lines were meant to stay!

We were ever ready to help a friend;
To offer aid; to give, to lend.

We welcomed the world, nor looked for flaws,
And all we asked, "Obey our laws".

I could tell of courage and faith through the years —
Things to inspire you, or move you to tears.

It is hard to choose, but the choice is mine —
That is what makes my country so fine!

In my freedom to write as I choose, I rejoice,
So, I'll tell of a people once given sad choice:

*The choice of renouncing French citizenship,*
*And swearing allegiance to England's king,*
*Or leaving their homes, their lands, all ties*
*That tilling and building and living can bring.*

## CHAPTER TWO

Now when and where shall my story start?
And when and where shall it end?
I'll start at its very beginning —
Have done when the story is penned.

So then I shall take you back to France,
In Sixteen Hundred and Four
When a band of French explorers sailed
To a distant, foreign shore.

They were men of valor, courage and dreams,
And their purpose was twofold:
To plant the Holy Cross and flag —
The New World's gift from the Old —

And to profit by a trade in furs,
Reports of which they had heard
Would help to fill French coffers.
Romance and Adventure stirred!

They were men of birth and breeding,
At ease with the sword or pen.
"Gentlemen of the Court" were they,
And "Soldiers of France" those men.

Among them was one Marc L'Escarbot,
(Unique was his place on the boat.)
A lawyer, he went as historian,
And 'twas he who later on wrote

"The History of New France", a book
That was published in Sixteen Nine.
Dedicated to the King and Court,
It was placed on sale at "The Sign

Of The Golden Compass", in Paris,
Where men might pause and read
Of the great exploits of their countrymen,
And many a noble deed.

Ah, great were those first adventurers
Sailing off to establish a claim;
And they held a king's commission
That was issued in the name

Of explorer, Pierre De Monts,
By Henry the Fourth of France.
De Monts was a man ever ready
His country's cause to advance.

With the hardy Samuel de Champlain,
He gathered men and supplies;
He needed only the strong and brave
To help him colonize.

So, he advertised, and from Normandy,
From Breton, and Brittany came
Good strong stock — from the coasts of France —
Not seeking wealth or fame,

For farmers they were, and fishermen,
In search of a livelihood,
And landing at last on a rock-bound coast,
All thought what they found was good.

"Acadia" they named the land,
(Marshland, highland, and spray)
"Port Royal" they called their settlement,
And there they planned to stay.

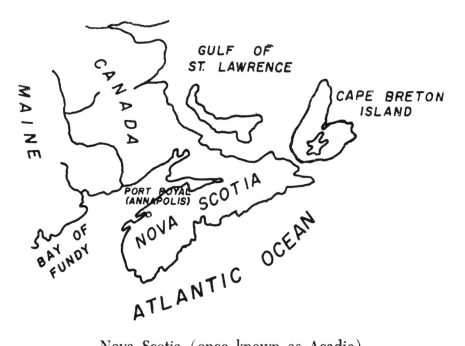

Nova Scotia (once known as Acadie)
Land from which the Acadians came.

## CHAPTER THREE

Blue, blue were the tall hill summits,
And lovely beyond compare;
Fertile and fair were the valleys,
The coast lines rugged and bare.

Only the Micmac Indians
Were there to welcome give —
Together with sky and trees,
In this land where they'd come to live.

They settled, and set about to wrest
A living from land and sea,
And where the trappers laid their lines
There was none to disagree.

The farmers cleared and tilled their farms,
Unrestricted and unoppressed;
The fishermen fished in waters deep,
With boundaries limitless.

Their low marsh lands reclaimed by dikes
Gave forth a goodly yield,
And bounteous was the harvest
From each man's well-tilled field.

Their summer months were very fair,
Their winters cold and long,
And though their leisure hours were few,
Those few they filled with song.

## CHAPTER FOUR

So passed the years until it seemed
Their happiness was secure.
Their homes were modest and unadorned,
Their home life simple and pure.

Hard-working, frugal, thrifty,
They asked but to be let alone.
Independent and self-sufficient,
The Acadians took care of their own.

Their communal life near perfect,
Each man seemed his brother's keeper.
Misfortune could strike with suddenness —
The stronger would help the weaker;

Would give from his overflowing barns
Or would help a home rebuild,
Till "Arcadia" seemed a likelier name,
So idyllic their lives, and so filled

With the simple joy of work well done,
And sharing a brother's labor;
With the joy of home and family,
And knowing and trusting his neighbor.

Their days were filled with a quiet content,
Of the World they were unaware;
They dreamed of a future made secure
By their efforts of work — and prayer.

## CHAPTER FIVE

But Fate had other things in store for them —
Their country failed with England to agree;
Acadia thereafter was but pawn
On Europe's chessboard of diplomacy.

Two mighty kings waged war and counter war;
Two alternating flags went up and down —
(The French and English flags) — above Port Royal,
That little, far-off, French provincial town.

Oft times did rival England gain control,
As oft' did France regain her rightful own,
Then Seventeen Thirteen saw a treaty signed,
(King Louis the Fourteenth occupied the throne),

The Treaty of Utrecht, it was called,
And France, exhausted by her wars, agreed
To cede Acadia to the English Crown.
Ah, was there none that day to intercede!

And so that long-contested tract of land
Came through its people's grief to know renown,
(A grief occasioned by their stern resolve
To not renounce allegiance to their Crown).

In later years a poet by pity moved,
Wrote touchingly with beauty of their trials.
*Evangeline*, Longfellow's poem, still lives,
And with each reading bridges years and miles.

# CHAPTER SIX

Poor Acadia, poor Acadians,
Who had, it seemed, once found the long-sought clue
Of living unoppressed by many fears;
Of having life's great dream of peace come true!

Throughout their land they'd found no need for locks.
They did not seek another's land or wealth,
Nor covet any neighbor's hard-earned store.
They did but pray for peace, long life, and health.

They nothing knew of politics and trends,
So of their coming loss they could not know —
That even their few, brief hours of song,
And their land's sweet name itself would go.

Sufficient to themselves they'd gone their way.
Their lives were such they could not understand
How other men could war continually —
How one man could invade another's land.

So doubly hard was turmoil when it came,
With terms of "traitor", "traitor to the king",
And unprepared were they for censure, blame,
Since they had asked for naught. Not anything,

Except to keep their homes and faith intact,
And so live out their quiet, secluded days;
To hold the land they felt to be their own,
Unhampered by intrusion, or strange ways.

Though France had lost her long and costly war,
And England owned the land where then they dwelt,
Through neutral pact with England they had gained
Immunity from war — or so they felt.

This pact they'd signed some forty years before —
Had promised not to fight on either side
In any English, French, or Indian war;
And practice of their faith was not denied.

Throughout the years this pact was questioned oft,
But always in the end it would suffice.
And then one day a Governor new and stern,
And harsh and unrelenting, asked a price.

Devout and proud and fiercely independent,
This price they felt they simply could not pay.
Concernedly they questioned one another,
Then asked themselves, how could they disobey

The promptings of their hearts that told them "No"?
Or the dictates of their conscience? They were loath,
Both by their race and deep religious fervor,
To take the stern and "unconditional oath"—

An oath that meant allegiance to a king
Other than their own. And, too, they saw
The practice of their Faith as circumscribed
"Within the limits of the English law."

Swear allegiance to the British Crown?
Forsake their King? There could be found
Along Acadia's rock-bound coast
No man who felt himself not honor bound

To voice refusal of this monstrous thing.
Divide a man's allegiance — what survives?
For loyalty to their faith, homeland, and king,
Made up the very pattern of their lives.

————————

THUS BRITAIN'S ULTIMATUM TO A NATION:
ACCEPT OUR TERMS, OR FACE EXPATRIATION.

## CHAPTER SEVEN

In all recorded history there has been
No choice more difficult for men to make
Than that made by those brave Acadians who
Accepted exile rather than forsake

Their heritage as citizens of France.
With anguished, stricken hearts they turned and left
Their homes, their lands, friendship and family ties —
Of all possessions shorn — bereaved, bereft.

With courage undismayed they made their choice,
Abandoned all they'd gained through lives of toil —
Their churches, and each hallowed resting place
Of those they'd loved. These bound them to the soil.

## CHAPTER EIGHT

Of what gain now? What purpose served, to dwell
On all the evils of expatriation?
Suffice to say those staunch Acadians bore
With boundless courage each trial and tribulation.

The dismal year was Seventeen Fifty-five
We learn, when history's ancient page we scan;
And their expulsion only further proves
Man's inhumanity to man.

And so we'll look aside, and draw the curtain to,
Until the last one leaves his stricken land —
All martyrs in their country's cause were they,
Their sacrifice endured for noble stand.

## CHAPTER NINE

Like sere, brown leaves they were scattered,
As though tossed by a wind on high,
That aimlessly carried them off,
Then as aimlessly dropped from the sky.

Or so it seemed to those careworn souls,
Bewildered and sick at heart.
What awaited them at their journey's end?
Strange customs, strange faces . . . a mart

Where no one would speak their native tongue.
How then would they living earn?
How worship and build, and dream of the things
For which each heart *must* yearn?

## CHAPTER TEN

Years passed, and weary their wanderings,
And harsh was the treatment received;
Nowhere were they welcomed, or wanted,
But still they went on . . . and believed.

Then a band of the more courageous,
Who were willing to take a chance,
Who had heard of Louisiana,
Then under the banner of France,

Had a dream of joining their countrymen there,
Under soft, blue southern skies;
To those poor, tired, alien outcasts
'Twas a dream of Paradise.

## Chapter Eleven

And so they set off on a long, long trip,
And traversing the continent,
They reached the Mississippi at last,
And there, with courage unspent

They launched their craft on its mighty tide
And finally reached their goal —
New Orleans — the City of Sympathy.
Did they vision an aureole?

For there they were quickly and kindly received,
And there once again they heard
The soft accents of their native tongue,
But what most touched — most stirred,

Was to find again their beloved Church,
After many long years of exile —
Ten years of incredible suffering,
And many a weary mile.

There, too, they found food and shelter,
The warm handclasp of a friend,
And an endless procession of sunlit days,
Going on and on without end;

The gentle tones of the Padre's voice,
Pity for the homeless and poor;
Compassion and understanding —
Could any man ask for more?

And then they were told of a wonderful place
On the banks of the beautiful Teche,
Where land could be tilled the full year 'round,
And flowers were always fresh.

No rock-bound coasts, no snow-bound months,
No fields that were frozen and bare,
No living hard and precarious,
No dikes needing constant repair,

But a place where land would be plentiful,
Where livestock, food, and supplies,
Would be furnished, and they could build churches,
And homes, under peaceful skies.

Ah, could it be possible, now, that they,
Refugees, unwanted so long,
Could even be given grants of land?
Could again use the word "belong"?

"I *belong* to this land. It is my home,
And this land *belongs* to me;
I will with its help a living earn
For myself and my family."

But ere they set off they went to church.
There they knelt and thanked their Lord,
For this they felt, was their answered prayer,
And this was their great reward!

## CHAPTER TWELVE

And so, they went back to the land again,
And the land a welcome gave.
Ah, there was a paradise, indeed,
Where a man could work and save!

They settled along the Bayou Teche,
With its soil and climate ideal,
Where the beauty of stream and tree and sky,
All nature set out to reveal.

And along the banks of Bayou Lafourche,
That lovely, slow-winding stream,
Still other Acadians came and found
Fulfillment of their dream.

Some sought the Mississippi's banks,
Later known as "Acadian Coast".
To a total of over four thousand
The State's south lands played host.

They sowed and they reaped and they prospered,
And offered thanks in His name;
They counted their blessings, forgetting not
The Source from which it all came.

They cut down forests and builded homes,
That were durable, lasting, and strong;
Hand-hewn were their logs, mud-plastered,
Put together with pegs and a song.

For they were a light-hearted people,
Impulsive, generous and warm;
They asked but little, demanded nought,
And sought not to injure or harm.

Well pleased were they with their own safe world,
Encompassed by home and friends,
And well content if a season's work
Would suffice for nature's ends.

And there, preserving their national traits,
Their customs, religion, and speech,
(Those qualities that distinguished them,
And which in turn they would teach

To generations who followed),
They lived out their well-rounded days,
Holding fast to their primitive virtues,
And their time-tested, Old-World ways.

## CHAPTER THIRTEEN

And so, they grew up with America,
This land of the Red, White and Blue;
Wrote one of its very first chapters,
And one of its finest, too.

Disappointed they'd been, when first they came
And found to their great dismay
That the King of Spain had supplanted their King,
And their flag would be taken away.

But the Spanish rule was to prove quite wise,
It would alter no law, nor name;
The speech of France would predominate,
The religion remain the same.

Undreamed of then was the United States,
To which they would one day be sold,
And as yet unborn was Napoleon,
Who would barter their land for gold.

But before that sale the land would go back
Under rule of France once again,
Though the flag would not be the Bourbon flag,
But the French Republic then.

And only for twenty days would it fly
In New Orleans' balmy air,
Over history-making, old Place d'Armes,
Now known as Jackson Square.

For the "LOUISIANA PURCHASE" treaty
Would be signed in Eighteen Three,
And the Acadians by that pen stroke
Become everlastingly free!

Would become not subjects, but citizens,
In their newly adopted land;
Would become *Americans,* quick to defend
*Their* country on every hand.

Ah, yes, they grew up with America,
This land of the Red, White, and Blue,
Wrote one of its very *first* chapters,
And one of its *finest,* too!

## Chapter Fourteen

Two hundred years and more have slipped away,
Since to our land the first Acadians came,
Bringing their dower of courage, but best of all —
What each prized most — his good Acadian name.

Two hundred years of progress and of growth —
Of growing with a country strong and young,
Of taking root, and being part of all
The upward sweep and climbing, rung by rung.

Those centuries have now become the past,
In Time's unhurried, even-measured flow.
*Le Grand Derangément* now, is but a tale
A thing that happened once, long, long ago.

And yet, in every walk of life today,
Acadian names add dignity and weight
To pulpit, education, politics,
To bench and bar, and service for the State.

As citizens they have contributed
Their share of worth to science, art and war;
They've recognition won for leadership,
And heroism shown — both near and far.

For amity and peaceable intentions,
By precept and example they are known,
But when in times of need their country calls,
They quickly rally to defend their own.

As part of the American Adventure,
The Acadians have played their part, and well,
Their influence for good, for Christian living,
Is found in every region where they dwell.

Any portrait of "America Today"
Bears imprint of Acadian life and charm,
For all their old traditions and romance,
Are treasured still as part of home and farm.

Their story now a legend has become,
A blend of faith, and courage of pioneer,
The patina of age but luster gives,
And adds unto its brightness year by year.

# L'ENVOI

And now my story is ended,
I open my window wide,
The morning star is silver bright,
The dawn unfolds outside.

The dawn — like a glorious omen,
O'er the heavens is brightly spread,
Foretelling with light and color
The future that lies ahead.

———————

Another two hundred years shall pass,
Another day shall dawn,
Another poem — another poet —
Acadia shall go on!

# HISTORICAL SKETCH

Acadia, now known as Nova Scotia, a peninsula extending off the extreme east coast of Canada, was first settled by the French in 1604. The Acadians were a worthy, happy, and industrious people, and in their new environs were engaged principally in farming, cattle raising, trapping and fishing. At no point in their new peninsula home were they ever more than fifty miles from the sea.

During the years that followed the coming of these French settlers to the western world, France and England were often at war with each other, their respective flags frequently alternating above Port Royal in Acadia.

At last in 1713, France, under the Treaty of Utrecht, ceded Acadia to England. Thereafter, from time to time, attempts were made to induce the Acadians to sign the oath of allegiance to England's King. This the Acadians could not bring themselves to do, and so it was that in 1755, after their final refusal to sign an "unconditional oath", which the Acadians believed would not only nullify their French citizenship, but would also "limit" the practice of their religion, they were forcibly evicted from their homes and farms, placed upon transports and scattered among the English colonies along the Atlantic seaboard.

For years following the exiling of the French inhabitants, the lot of the refugees, speaking a foreign tongue, was a sad and harsh one. Some sought desperately hard to return to their Acadian homeland. A number of them, after ten years of incredible hardship, finally reached New Orleans by way of the Mississippi River. At New Orleans, though the territory at the time was under Spanish domination, they were given welcome. There, too, they were furnished with food, farming implements, live stock, and even given grants of land along the banks of the Bayou Teche, and the Attakapas prairies to the north and west. These first Acadians were followed by still others who settled along Bayou Lafourche. A large number sought refuge along the banks of the Mississippi River in a section above New Orleans that came to be known as the Acadian Coast.

In their new locations they cut down trees, cleared the land, built homes and planted crops and, as in their beloved Acadia, earned a livelihood by farming, cattle raising and fishing. In addition they added to their income by trapping in the rich, fur-bearing bayous of southern Louisiana. It is estimated that fully four thousand Acadians sought refuge in south Louisiana.

The Acadians proved to be peaceful, law-abiding citizens, loyal to their new country. Especially were they noted for their love of home and family. Though today the descendants of the Acadians can be found in all strata of society, many having attained positions of wealth and distinction, and are scattered throughout the entire country, a large number of the descendants of the original settlers are still located in and near the cities where their ancestors first settled. There, many are still engaged in the early occupations of their forefathers, farming, trapping, cattle raising and fishing.

NOTE—"Acadie", the original spelling of the Acadians' homeland was later changed by the British to "Nova Scotia", meaning New Scotland.

# TIME PASSES–TIME CHANGES–TIME HEALS

Today there stands in Nova Scotia, on a once oft-contested, historic battle cite, a tall granite monument surmounted by a bronze bust of Pierre de Monts of France which was erected in 1904 by Canada on fort grounds, to commemorate the 300th anniversary of the founding of Port Royal. The inscription reads as follows:

"To the illustrious Memory of Lieut. Gen'l Timothe Pierre du Guast Sieur de Monts. The Pioneer of Civilization in North America Who Discovered and Explored The Adjacent River, A.D. 1604, and Founded on its Banks The First Settlement of Europeans North of the Gulf of Mexico. The Government of Canada reverently Dedicates This Monument Within Sight of That Settlement, A.D. 1904. Genus Immortale manet."

Map showing early Acadian settlements
in Louisiana